MEXICO
the land

Bobbie Kalman

A Bobbie Kalman Book

The Lands, Peoples, and Cultures Series

 Crabtree Publishing Company

www.crabtreebooks.com

The Lands, Peoples, and Cultures Series
Created by Bobbie Kalman

For Fruzan and Ian

Written by
Bobbie Kalman

Coordinating editor
Ellen Rodger

Editor
Jane Lewis

Contributing editors
Kate Calder
Carrie Gleason

Editor/first edition
David Schimpky

Production coordinator
Rose Gowsell

Design and production
Text Etc.

Separations and film
Quadratone Graphics Ltd.

Printer
Worzalla Publishing Company

Photographs
AFP/ Corbis/ Magmaphoto: p. 12 (inset); Annie G. Belt/Corbis/ Magmaphoto: p. 18 (top); Jim Bryant: p. 5 (inset), 8 (bottom), 9 (top), 14, 21 (top); Milt & Joan Mann/ Cameramann Int'l., Ltd.: p. 7 (top), 11 (both), 15, 18 (bottom), 20, 22 (bottom), 23 (top), 24, 25, 31 (top); Betty Crowell: p. 21 (bottom), 22 (top), 27 (bottom left), 30; Owen Franken/ Corbis / Magmaphoto: p. 10; Hollenbeck Photography: p. 7 (bottom), 8 (top), 29 (both); Wolfgang Kaehler: p. 31 (bottom); James Kamstra: p. 26 (top), 27 (top, bottom right); Roger Ressmeyer/ Corbis/ Magmaphoto: p.13; Superstock/ Steve Vidler: pages 16–17; other images by Digital Stock

Every effort has been made to obtain the appropriate credit and full copyright clearance for all images in this book. Any oversights, despite Crabtree's greatest precautions, will be corrected in future editions.

Map
Jim Chernishenko

Illustrations
Scott Mooney: icons
Bonna Rouse: p. 15
David Wysotski, Allure Illustrations: back cover

Cover: Agave plants are commonly found throughout Mexico.

Title page: Mayan ruins located all across Mexico reveal the complex civilizations that populated the country in ancient times.

Icon: Sonoran cactus

Back cover: The chihuahua is a type of small dog that was once kept by the native peoples of Mexico.

Published by
Crabtree Publishing Company

PMB 16A
350 Fifth Avenue
Suite 3308
New York
N.Y. 10118

612 Welland Avenue
St. Catharines
Ontario, Canada
L2M 5V6

73 Lime Walk
Headington
Oxford OX3 7AD
United Kingdom

Cataloging in Publication Data
Kalman, Bobbie, 1947-
    Mexico. The Land / Bobbie Kalman. - Rev. ed.
    p. cm. -- (The lands, peoples, and cultures series)
    Includes index.
    ISBN 0-7787-9361-3 (RLB) -- ISBN 0-7787-9729-5 (pbk.)
    1. Mexico -- Description and travel--Juvenile literature. 2. Mexico--Social conditions--Juvenile literature. 3. Mexico--Economic conditions--Juvenile literature. [1. Mexico.] I. Title. II. Series.
F1208.5 .K325 2002
972--dc21

2001028190
LC

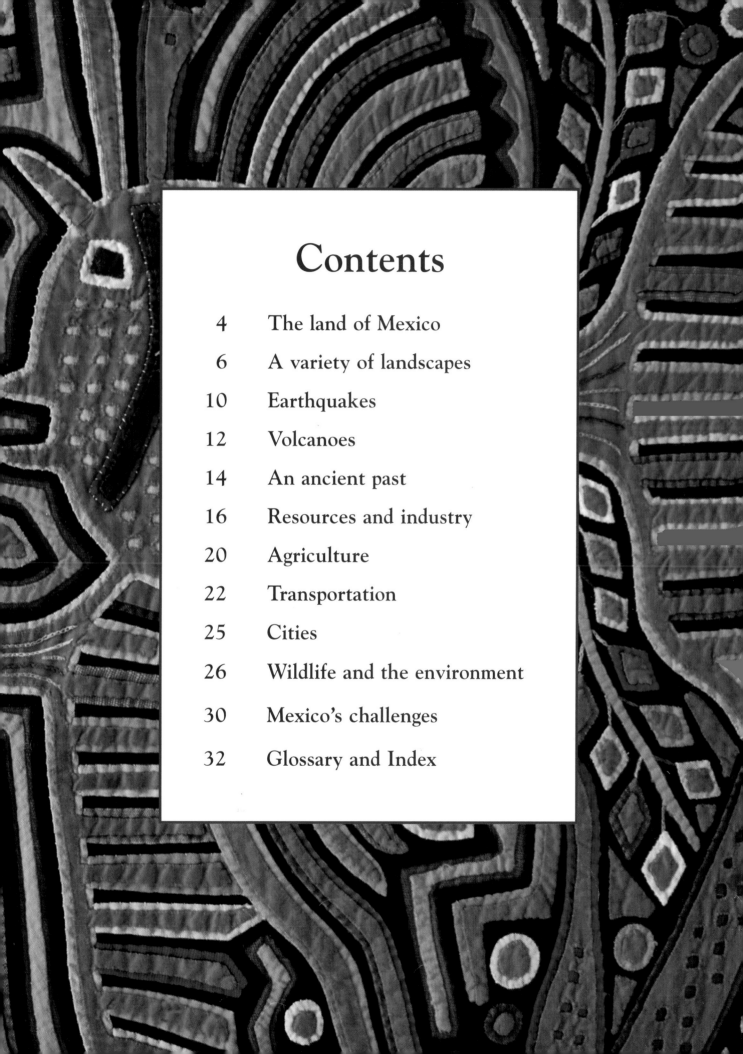

Contents

The land of Mexico

There is a legend about Hernán Cortés, the Spanish adventurer who conquered the Aztec civilization in Mexico. In 1528 he was called back to Spain to report on the **New World**. The king, curious about his new **empire**, asked him to describe the land of Mexico. Cortés picked up a piece of paper, crumpled it, and tossed it on a table. "This is Mexico," he said.

The gesture illustrated how mountainous the land of Mexico was, but Cortés failed to show the beauty and variety of the land with his demonstration. Mexico is dry deserts and lush rainforests; it is rolling hills and broad plains. Modern Mexico is also full of contrasts: there are factories and farms, huge cities and small towns, populated areas and untouched wilderness.

(right) Mexico's many hills make house building a challenging task!

(below) The Sierra Madre Occidental, the Sierra Madre Oriental, and the Neovolcanic Cordillera are the three main mountain regions of Mexico.

A variety of landscapes

(above) A long stretch of northwest desert showing the palm trees of an oasis.

Mexico is a North American country that shares its northern border with the United States. The country's southern border is shared with Guatemala and Belize. The North Pacific Ocean and the Gulf of California lie to the west of Mexico, and the Gulf of Mexico and the Caribbean Sea lie to the east. Mexico is divided into 31 states and one federal district, however, the country is more easily described in terms of its regions. The landscape, the vegetation, and the climate vary greatly from region to region.

Northwest deserts

Northwest Mexico, made up of Baja California and the states of Sonora and Sinaloa, is the most isolated part of the country. The land is dry, hot, and **barren**. Some deserts in this area have hardy vegetation, but others support little life. There is some vegetation around the Gulf of California, as well as a few **fertile** spots, called **oases**, which are fed by underground springs.

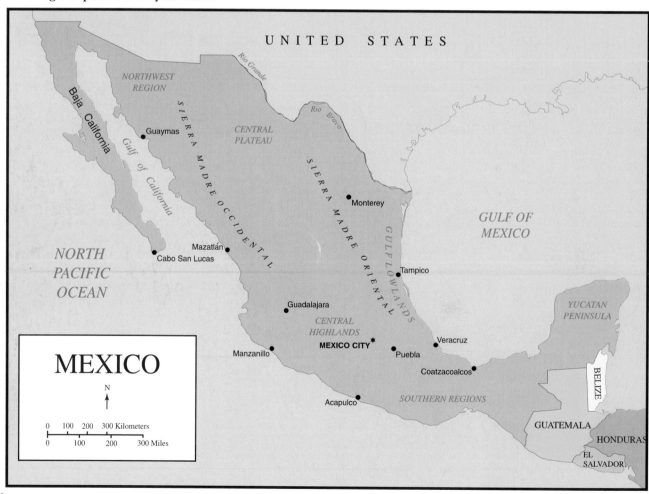

UNITED STATES

NORTHWEST REGION

Rio Grande

Rio Bravo

SIERRA MADRE OCCIDENTAL

CENTRAL PLATEAU

SIERRA MADRE ORIENTAL

GULF LOWLANDS

Baja California

Gulf of California

Guaymas

Monterey

GULF OF MEXICO

NORTH PACIFIC OCEAN

Mazatlán
Cabo San Lucas

Tampico

YUCATAN PENINSULA

Guadalajara

CENTRAL HIGHLANDS

MEXICO CITY★

Veracruz

Manzanillo

Puebla

Coatzacoalcos

BELIZE

MEXICO

N
↑

0   100   200   300 Kilometers
0   100   200   300 Miles

Acapulco

SOUTHERN REGIONS

GUATEMALA

HONDURAS

EL SALVADOR

The Central Plateau

Two long mountain ranges follow the Pacific and Gulf coasts of Mexico. To the west is the steep Sierra Madre Occidental, and to the east is the rolling Sierra Madre Oriental. Between these two ranges lies the Central **Plateau**. This high-altitude area is dry, although not as hot and dry as the northwest. It has few rivers or lakes. Mining, ranching, farming, and forestry are among the industries operating in this region.

The Central Highlands

The most heavily populated region in Mexico is the Central Highlands. This area sits on a high plateau, surrounded on three sides by mountains. To the east is the Sierra Madre Oriental mountain range. To the west is the Sierra Madre Occidental, and to the south is the Neovolcanic Cordillera. It is in this last range that you can find most of Mexico's volcanoes.

(above) The Central Plateau is a dry, high-altitude region with few rivers or lakes.

(above) Guanajuato is one of many cities located in the Central Highlands.

The tropical lowlands

The Gulf Lowlands follow the eastern coast of Mexico from Tamaulipas state to the state of Veracruz. This flat plain lies between the Gulf of Mexico and the Sierra Madre Oriental mountain range. Its tropical climate makes it an ideal home for many different kinds of plants and animals.

The mountainous south

In the Southern Region, winters are warm and dry, whereas summers are hot and **humid**. Several mountain ranges, including the Sierra Madre del Sur, the Sierra Madre de Oaxaca, and the Sierra de Soconusco are located in this region. Dry, **deciduous** forests still stand in some northern parts of this sparsely populated region. Thick rainforest makes up the vegetation in the southern Chiapas state. Unfortunately, heavy logging has destroyed many of the forested areas in the south.

(above) Tropical lowlands exist between the Sierra Madre Occidental mountains and the Pacific coast.

(below) Thick rainforest covers parts of southern Mexico.

The Yucatán Peninsula

The easternmost part of Mexico is the Yucatán **Peninsula**, which juts into the Gulf of Mexico. The Yucatán is a flat, low-lying **limestone** shelf covered by tropical forest. Limestone dissolves easily, so the peninsula is full of caverns and underground rivers. There are many sinkholes in this area. Sinkholes form when the ground between a cavern and the earth's surface grows too thin and collapses. Sinkholes can cause damage to buildings and roads.

Lakes and rivers

The majority of Mexico's lakes can be found in the Central Highlands. Lakes Chapala and Pátzcuaro are among the largest lakes in the country. Mexico's largest river is the Río Bravo del Norte, which forms part of the border between Mexico and the United States. People in the United States call this river the Rio Grande. Many rivers in Mexico have been dammed and used for hydroelectric projects. **Hydroelectricity** uses fast water to drive **turbines**. The turbines then create electrical power.

(above) Deep in the wilderness of Chiapas lies a waterfall called Cascada Agua Azul, which means "cascade of blue water."

(below) Lake Chapala, in the state of Jalisco in the Central Highlands region, is Mexico's largest lake.

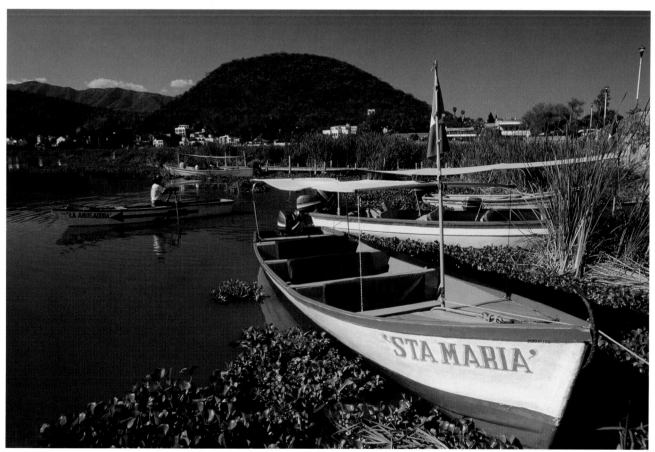

Earthquakes

Earthquakes are one of the world's most deadly natural disasters. Mexico has been shaken by earthquakes many times. One of the worst earthquakes hit Mexico City in 1985, killing over 10,000 people and leaving thousands more injured or homeless.

Protection from earthquakes

Scientists who study earthquakes are called seismologists. Seismologists try to find ways of predicting when and where an earthquake will strike. If scientists can warn of an earthquake in advance, people who live in the danger zone can then take safety precautions. During the 1985 earthquake, many buildings in Mexico City collapsed, killing thousands of people. New buildings are designed and built to be sturdy enough to withstand the violent tremors of an earthquake.

(above) This apartment building was destroyed by an earthquake's tremors.

(opposite page, top) Mexico's newer buildings are designed to withstand earthquakes.

(opposite page, bottom) Large waves are created when an earthquake takes place under the ocean.

Shifting plates

A theory called plate tectonics explains why there are so many earthquakes in Mexico. Scientists believe that the surface, or crust, of the earth is made up of several different pieces, called plates. These plates are constantly moving. Some move away from other plates, some move toward other plates, and some rub sideways against one another. In areas where the plates come together, the ground is unstable and often shakes with vibrations, called tremors. Severe tremors are called earthquakes. Mexico is located at a point where four plates meet. The shifting of these plates causes many earthquakes in Mexico.

Tsunami

Earthquakes that occur under the ocean can create a giant wave of water called a *tsunami*. These waves can be as high as one hundred feet (30 meters)! *Tsunamis* sometimes hit the west coast of Mexico and cause a great deal of damage and destruction to the shoreline.

Volcanoes

Volcanoes, like earthquakes, are found in areas where the plates of the earth's crust meet. Mexico is home to about 3,000 volcanoes, most of which are located in an area west of Mexico City. Some have names, such as Citlaltépetl and Popocatépetl, that date from Aztec times.

How volcanoes work

A volcano is a crack in the earth's crust. Hot, liquid rock, called magma, rises through the crack when a volcano erupts. When the magma reaches the surface, it is called lava. The lava cools and becomes rock. After many eruptions, layers of lava build up and form a high cone.

So many volcanoes

There are three types of volcanoes. Volcanoes that no longer erupt are called extinct. A volcano that has not erupted for a long time, but may still become active, is called dormant. If lava, ash, or smoke comes out of a volcano, that volcano is called active.

Iztaccíhuatl, Mexico's legendary volcano (see next page), is an extinct volcano. The Pico de Orizaba, 60 miles (97 kilometers) east of the city of Puebla, is a dormant volcano. It is 18,406 feet (5610 meters) high and is Mexico's highest mountain. In the Aztec language, it is called Citlaltépetl, which means "star mountain." Fuego de Colima, in the state of Guadalajara, is one of the most active volcanoes in the world. It has erupted 30 times in the past 400 years.

Eruption!

Some volcanic eruptions happen very slowly, but many are violent and can quickly destroy surrounding areas. A violent eruption occurs when the top of a volcano is sealed with cooled lava. The pressure within the volcano builds until the volcano suddenly bursts, expelling gas, steam, ash, rock fragments, and rivers of lava. Fortunately, scientists are learning more about volcanoes. They hope to be able to predict when a volcano will erupt, so people who live nearby can seek safety.

Volcano of the warrior

There is an Aztec legend about the volcano called Popocatépetl and a nearby mountain called Iztaccíhuatl. There was once a princess and a mighty warrior who were in love. One day there was a great battle in which the warrior was victorious. Unfortunately, his enemies sent word to the princess that the warrior was dead, and she died of a broken heart. When the warrior returned and heard the news, he was very sad. In his grief, he built two great mountains. He placed the princess's body on the mountain called Iztaccíhuatl, which means "sleeping woman." He then stood on the volcano of Popocatépetl, which means "smoking mountain," holding a torch lit in her memory.

Popocatépetl today

Popocatépetl is located 45 miles (72 kilometers) from Mexico City. Although this volcano has not fully erupted since 1702, it was active again in recent years. There have been many minor eruptions, sending smoke, ash, and steam into the air. Some scientists think that Popocatépetl may fully erupt soon.

Mexico's youngest volcano

In 1943, a volcano appeared in the middle of a farmer's field—much to the farmer's surprise! The volcano was named Paricutín. It grew rapidly, and was active for nine years before becoming dormant. Paricutín eventually reached a height of 9,210 feet (2,808 meters). This volcano is one of the youngest volcanoes in the world. Paricutín has given scientists a rare opportunity to observe a volcano through its various stages of development.

(above) Fuego de Colima is located in the state of Colima on the western coast of Mexico.

(opposite page, inset) Popocatépetl has been active in recent years. This eruption took place in December 2000.

(opposite page, bottom) Although it is an active volcano, the summit of Popocatépetl is covered year-round by snow.

 # An ancient past

People were living in North America long before Europeans "discovered" the continent. It is believed that, as many as 40,000 years ago, people from Asia crossed a sandbar or an ice bridge in the **Bering Strait** to Alaska. By 20,000 B.C., some of these people had **migrated** as far south as Mexico. Several of these groups developed into advanced **civilizations**.

The Olmecs

The Olmecs were the first major civilization in Mexico. They built villages and **monuments** in the thick forests of the eastern coast between 1500 B.C. and 200 B.C. **Archaeologists** have uncovered a site, called San Lorenzo, that the Olmecs may have used for religious ceremonies. The most striking features of San Lorenzo are huge heads that are carved from rock. Some of these heads are over nine feet (three meters) tall!

Complex cultures

The Zapotec, Mixtec, and Mayan cultures flourished at various times between 600 B.C. and 1500 A.D. Cities consisting of pyramids, temples, and homes were built across Mexico. People in these native civilizations gained much knowledge of the natural world. They also recorded their history and spiritual beliefs. Southern Mexico was dotted with cities built by the Zapotecs. The Mixtecs lived in the nearby mountain regions. A huge **metropolis** called Teotihuacán dominated central Mexico. Mayan cities were built across the Yucatán Peninsula and Central America. The city of Teotihuacán was abandoned and the Mayan civilization declined by 900 A.D. The reason is still a mystery. Today, all that remains of the great cities are archaeological sites and ruins covered by thick rainforest.

The Aztecs

After the decline of Teotihuacán, several native groups such as the Toltecs, Totonacs, Huastecs, and Tarascans lived throughout Mexico. A group known as the Aztecs eventually conquered many of the other native peoples. The Aztecs built an empire that stretched across central and southern Mexico. The center of their empire was a large city called Tenochtitlán, which was built on an island in Lake Texcoco. Modern-day Mexico City is built over the Aztec capital, and several temples and pyramids are still standing.

Spanish conquest

Mexico's native culture changed in 1519 when Hernán Cortés landed on the Gulf coast of Mexico. The Spanish adventurer had heard stories of a kingdom of riches and came with 400 soldiers. The Aztecs were disliked by other native groups, and Cortés found plenty of allies to help fight them. By 1521 the Aztec ruler Moctezuma II (also spelled Montezuma) had been killed, and Spain had taken control. The Spanish claimed the country as part of their empire, and named it New Spain. At that time, Mexico included territory that now belongs to the United States and Central America.

(above) Ruins of the Aztec city Tenochtitlán, a colonial Spanish church, and modern apartment buildings can be seen at the Plaza of the Three Cultures in Mexico City.

(opposite page) The city of Palenque in Chiapas contains some of the best-preserved Mayan buildings in Mexico.

Aztec leader Moctezuma greets Spanish explorer Hernán Cortés.

Moctezuma and the Spaniards

Quetzalcoatl was considered a powerful Aztec god. The Aztec people believed he had gone away but would one day return. At the time that Quetzalcoatl's return was expected, the Aztecs heard rumors of strange creatures approaching from the north. The Aztec people wondered if these strangers might be the god Quetzalcoatl and his followers. When he saw the pale-faced men, the Aztec leader Moctezuma II greeted the one he thought was Quetzalcoatl and offered him the city of Tenochtitlán. Too late, the Aztecs learned that Quetzalcoatl and his followers were actually the explorer Hernán Cortés and his army. Although the Aztecs fought to regain their city, Tenochtitlán was lost. The Spanish destroyed the city and built Mexico City on its ruins.

Resources and industry

Mexico is rich in **natural resources** such as oil, natural gas, minerals, and precious metals. Some of these resources are used by Mexican people; some are sold to other countries. Another natural resource is Mexico's good weather and beautiful landscapes. These have contributed to a profitable tourism industry.

Mexico is one of the most industrialized countries in **Latin America**. Many factories have been built in Mexico so that the owners can benefit from low energy costs, tax breaks, and the low wages paid to Mexican workers. In addition to manufacturing and tourism, steel production, mining, oil, natural gas, fishing, and forestry are important industries.

(below) Fishing crews on Lake Pátzcuaro in the Central Highlands still use wide butterfly nets, named for their shape. This fishing method has been used for generations.

Oil

Oil is important to Mexico's economy. The first oil wells were developed in 1901. Within twenty years, Mexico was one of the world's greatest oil-producing nations. Today, all of Mexico's oil fields are managed by Pemex, which stands for Petróleos Mexicanos. Pemex is owned by the government and controls all aspects of Mexico's petroleum industry, including exploration, drilling, and export. Most of Mexico's oil fields lie along the east coast. Huge oil-drilling platforms also extract this valuable resource from the ocean floor in the Gulf of Mexico.

Precious metals

The first minerals to be mined in Mexico were gold and silver. Silver mining in particular brought wealth to the Spanish **colonial** rulers. Mexico is still the world's largest producer of silver. The states of Guanajuato and San Luis Potosí in central Mexico are centers of silver mining operations.

Mineral mining

Iron **ore** is mined in the northern state of Durango and coal is mined in the neighboring state of Coahuila. The city of Monterrey is an important center for iron and steel production. Many other minerals, including copper, lead, zinc, sulfur, manganese, and uranium, are mined in Mexico.

Forestry

Although much of northern Mexico is too dry to support vast forests, there are wooded areas on the slopes of the Sierra Madres. Many of these pine and white cedar forests have been cut down to provide firewood and charcoal for neighboring towns and villages. Some of the lumber is used in construction, furniture, and paper industries. Many of the thick forests in southern Mexico, filled with mahogany, cedar, oak, and evergreen trees, have also been chopped down for lumber.

Fishing

The majority of the Mexican fishing industry is located along the Pacific coast. In the Gulf of California, fishing crews haul in great quantities of lobster, sardines, anchovies, shrimp, and tuna. Most of the catch is exported to the United States. The Gulf of Mexico and the Caribbean Sea also teem with a variety of fish, including shrimp, trout, flounder, **tarpon**, tuna, mackerel, and red snapper. Pearls are gathered from oysters in the Gulf. Many fishing crews on Mexico's inland lakes still use traditional fishing methods, such as wide butterfly nets, for scooping fish from the lakes.

High-tech manufacturing

Mexico City and northern Mexico are large centers for high-tech manufacturing. Along the Mexico-United States border, there are many factories called *maquiladoras*, which are owned by foreign companies. These factories operate close to the border because most of the manufactured products are exported back to the United States. Steel, chemicals, television sets, computers, clothing, and other items are produced in these factories. Cars and trucks are assembled at plants located in northwest Mexico.

(top) . The employees in this factory are assembling circuit boards. The majority of factory workers in Mexico are women.

(bottom) Many Mexican factories produce clothing that is exported to other countries. These workers are putting the finishing touches on the shoes that are made in this factory.

(opposite page) The beaches of Cancún in the Yucatán attract many foreign tourists. Tourism is important to Mexico's economy.

Free trade

The North American Free Trade Agreement (NAFTA) was introduced in 1994. This agreement reduced the amount of tax that Mexico, the United States, and Canada have to pay when they trade goods with one another. NAFTA has encouraged more trading between the three countries, which helps the economy of each country. Many new factories have been built in Mexico because of NAFTA, and this has created jobs for Mexican workers.

Visiting Mexico

Each winter, millions of tourists visit Mexico, mostly from the United States and Canada. The tourism industry is extremely important to the country. It brings billions of dollars to the economy and employs millions of people. Ancient ruins, historic sites, cultural attractions, warm weather, beach resorts, and low prices make Mexico a favorite vacation destination for many travelers.

Not enough jobs

Despite its many industries, NAFTA, and plentiful natural resources, Mexico has a high unemployment rate. There are simply too many people and not enough jobs. Wages remain low because there are so many people available to work. It is difficult to make a living in rural areas because there is not much land available to farm. Many people have moved from the country to large cities, such as Mexico City, to look for work. Unfortunately, there are not enough jobs in the cities for all the newcomers.

Crossing the border

Some Mexicans **emigrate** to the United States and find work there. Others cross the border and work illegally because they have no other way to make money. Illegal workers in the United States often live and work in poor conditions and make little money. Illegal workers have no legal rights, so if they demand fair treatment they could lose their jobs.

 # Agriculture

Agriculture has always been one of Mexico's most important industries. Before 1910, most farming was done on *haciendas*, or ranches. Some of these large farms were millions of acres in size. The wealthy owners employed peasants to work the land. They paid the peasants low wages and forced them to live in difficult conditions. This injustice caused a **revolution** by the Mexican people in 1910.

Sharing the land

A new **constitution** was written in 1917. It stated the laws that would govern Mexico. One law made the *haciendas* illegal. The land was distributed to the peasants, who were allowed to work the land as if it were their own. The peasants could not sell their land, but they could pass it on to their children. In 1992, the government passed a law that allowed farmers to buy and sell their own land.

Communal farms

In the past, small groups of farmers often banded together to form large communal, or shared, farms called *ejidos*. The *ejido* system was supported by the Mexican government for many years. Today, *ejidos* have started to disappear. Often, Mexican farmers lack the agricultural training and equipment to be successful. Few farmers have enough money for new, modern equipment. As well, most farms are small and cannot produce enough to survive. Many farmers have sold their land to large farm owners and moved to urban areas to look for work. Despite these changes, one out of four Mexicans work in the agriculture industry.

Little land to farm

Only one-fifth of the land in Mexico is suitable for farming—the rest is either mountainous or dry and rocky. With the help of **irrigation**, cotton and wheat are now major crops in northern Mexico. Sheep and cattle ranching also take place in the north. The best farmland in the country is located in the southern part of the Central Plateau region. Many crops, including corn, beans, and rice are grown there. In the tropical south, bananas, mangoes, citrus fruits, sugarcane, avocados, vanilla, and coffee are grown. Coffee, cotton, tomatoes, and many types of fruit are exported to other countries.

Corn, beans, and squash

The most important crops grown for consumption in Mexico are corn, beans, and squash. Corn, or *maíze*, is a major part of each Mexican's diet. It is usually ground and made into flat breads called *tortillas*. Beans, called *frijoles*, are often cooked, then mashed and fried. Squash can be cooked many ways—boiled, baked, or fried. Mexicans do not eat much meat. These three vegetables provide the important vitamins and **protein** needed in a person's diet.

(opposite page) This farmer is harvesting prickly pear cactus branches. They can be cooked and eaten like a vegetable.

(right) Centuries-old farming techniques are still used by many native farmers. As a result, their farms are not as profitable as more modern farms.

(bottom) These workers are employed on a large-scale tomato farm. The long plastic sheets protect the delicate young tomato plants from the wind.

21

 # Transportation

A trip across Mexico can be a challenge because of the mountainous countryside. Traveling in large cities can also be difficult because of the number of vehicles using the roads. Cars, buses, bicycles, trains, and airplanes are just some of the forms of transportation used in Mexico.

The railroad

There are 19,293 miles (31,048 kilometers) of railroad track crisscrossing Mexico. Most of the railways were built between 1876 and 1910. In recent years, many trains have stopped running because they were not making any money. Most Mexican businesses consider the railroad slow and inefficient. They prefer to use trucks to transport their goods. Passengers also prefer to travel by road instead of rail.

(above) Despite Mexico's 19,293 miles of railroad track, automobiles are the preferred method of transportation for people and products.

Roads and highways

Over the last 50 years, the number of paved highways has increased greatly. There are now more than 55,000 miles (88,550 kilometers) of highway in Mexico. Remote areas, such as Baja California and the Yucatán Peninsula, can now be reached by trucks and automobiles. Trucks are an important means of transport for Mexican industries. Bus lines connecting major cities are a popular and easy way for Mexicans to travel to other parts of the country.

Ocean ports

Mexico's largest ports are at the cities of Tampico, Veracruz, Guaymas, Mazatlán, and Manzanillo. Coatzacoalcos and Acapulco are also important ports. At one time, Mexico's ocean ports were owned and operated by the government. Many businesses found the ports old fashioned and costly to use. Many ports have been sold to private companies. Private ownership has greatly improved the Mexican shipping industry.

(left) Millions of people driving cars in Mexican cities results in constant traffic jams.

In the air

Air travel in Mexico increased greatly toward the end of the last century. Airports were built and improved in order to handle the large numbers of tourists visiting the country. Mexico's two largest national airlines are Aeroméxico and Mexicana, and there are many other smaller airlines in operation.

Rural transportation

In some of the more remote parts of Mexico, people rely on forms of transportation that have been used for centuries. **Burros**, horses, and oxen are used to pull carts, carry riders, and drag plows. People often walk from place to place. Many people in these areas do not have the money to buy tractors or automobiles.

In the city

Many forms of transportation can be seen in Mexico's cities. People use cars, buses, taxis, bicycles, motorcycles, and subways to get from place to place. Goods are transported mainly by trucks, although animals pulling carts can sometimes be spotted amidst the traffic.

(above) Burros are still a cheap, reliable form of transportation in Mexico.

(below) Cabo San Lucas, at the southern tip of Baja California, is one of Mexico's many ports.

Cities

At the beginning of the twentieth century, nine out of ten Mexicans lived in rural areas. By the beginning of the twenty-first century, this had changed dramatically. Now, the majority of Mexican people live in cities.

Massive Mexico City

With a population of more than twenty million people and growing, Mexico City is one of the largest cities in the world. One out of four Mexicans live there! It is the capital of Mexico and the center of Mexico's industry, business, and culture. Mexico City is one of the oldest cities in North America. It was established in 1521 as the capital of the Spanish empire in North America. Mexico City was built over the site of the ancient Aztec capital of Tenochtitlán.

Guadalajara

Mexico's second largest city is Guadalajara. This city has been important in the development of western Mexico. Many beautiful churches and houses, as well as museums and a university, were built there. Guadalajara is a center of music and industry. Two major industries are the manufacturing of ceramics and an alcoholic drink called tequila.

Monterrey

The northern city of Monterrey, the third largest city in Mexico, is a center of business. Many corporations and industries are located there, including huge steel mills. Monterrey is also home to three large universities. The most famous is the Monterrey Institute of Technology and Higher Education, which trains Mexican students in the sciences.

Growing pains

Each year, thousands of Mexicans move from the countryside to find jobs in urban centers. The cities must provide housing, sanitation, and education for new residents. Poverty, traffic jams, pollution, and overcrowding are major problems in Mexico's big urban centers.

(opposite page) Monumento a la Independencia, a symbol of Mexico City, is known to many Mexicans as "The Angel."

(below) Guadalajara is a modern city located near Lake Chapala. Its citizens enjoy mild, sunny weather all year round.

Wildlife and the environment

Just as Mexico's landscape varies from region to region, so does the wildlife. Each region is home to many species of plants and animals. Some of these species are not found anywhere else in the world! Scientists have determined that Mexico is one of the few places on earth where millions of different kinds of plants and animals can live.

Refuge in the desert

The deserts of northwest Mexico and Baja California are home to animals such as the desert tortoise and the poisonous Gila monster. The remote hills of the Baja peninsula are a **refuge** for the desert bighorn sheep and hunting grounds for the puma. Almost one thousand types of cacti grow in Mexico's deserts. Yucca plants, agaves, mesquite, and many kinds of grasses also grow in these areas.

Mountains and highlands

Small animals such as rabbits, snakes, badgers, and armadillos are common in Mexico's mountainous and plateau regions. Birds such as eagles, hawks, and vultures, and larger animals such as deer, bears, coyotes, sheep, wolves, and mountain lions can also be found. These areas were once covered by pine and oak forests, but many trees have been cut down by the logging industry.

(above) The colors of the helmeted basilisk help it blend in with the leaves and branches of Mexico's forests.

(left) The agave plant is common in the northern desert areas of Mexico.

(opposite page, top) The coatamundi loves climbing trees to find fruit, eggs, and insects to eat.

(opposite page, bottom left) Many kinds of colorful birds such as this macaw live in Mexico's jungles.

(opposite page, bottom right) It may look ferocious, but this kind of bat eats only fruit.

The forests of the south

Evergreen tropical forests and rainforests can be found in southern Mexico. Mahogany, cedar, and fruit trees such as mango, papaya, and banana grow in the rainforests. Sapodilla trees, which produce chicle, a product used to make chewing gum, also grow in the south. Mexico's southern forests are home to many varieties of animals. The black howler monkey and the spider monkey live in the jungles, as do **tapirs**, anteaters, parrots, boa constrictors, and peccaries. Several species of cats, including the jaguar, **margay**, and **ocelot**, hunt in the wilderness areas. Flocks of brilliant pink flamingos fly over the swamps of the Yucatán. Vampire bats live in the sinkholes of that region.

Coastal waters

Sea turtles live on every coast in Mexico. Sea lions and harbor seals live off the coast of Baja California. Dolphins swim off the Pacific coast and in the Gulf of Mexico. Many types of whales live in Mexican waters. The gray whale spends its winters in the Gulf of California after migrating from its summer home in the Arctic Ocean. Sixty years ago, the gray whale was almost extinct due to overhunting. Today these animals are protected, and nearly 21,000 gray whales make the annual journey to Mexico.

A bevy of butterflies

Each winter, the eastern part of Michoacán state is swarmed by visitors from Canada and the United States. They are not tourists—they are monarch butterflies! These large, orange-and-black insects travel hundreds of miles each year to this spot. Sadly, the butterflies may be in danger because logging operations are destroying their forest **habitat**.

(above) Millions of monarch butterflies migrate to Mexico every year from the U.S. and Canada.

(below) Dolphins are some of the many marine animals that live in Mexican waters.

Disappearing forests

Much of Mexico's wildlife has been threatened by human activities such as logging and farming. Over the past several years, forests have been cut down at a rapid rate. Logging operations are part of the problem. Although logging has brought economic reward to some people, it has also meant the destruction of unique and beautiful wilderness areas. Farming is also to blame. Farmers have burned or chopped down forests to create more farmland. As a result, many plants and animals are endangered because they have lost their natural habitat.

Protected areas

People have begun to realize that it is important to protect the wildlife in Mexico. There are 64 national parks in the country, which protect some of the land. Unfortunately, many parks do not have the resources to prevent people from illegally logging or hunting inside their boundaries. Mexico also has 23 areas called **biosphere** reserves. These reserves protect areas in which many different species of plants and animals live. Local people are encouraged to use methods of farming, fishing, and logging that do not destroy the areas in which they work. This is called sustainable agriculture.

(top) The Sian Ka'an Biosphere Reserve is located on the Yucatán Peninsula. Tours of this reserve are carefully controlled so that the land and environment are preserved.

(bottom) Mexico's rainforests are full of valuable plants and animals that need to be protected.

Mexico's challenges

Mexico is a land of opposites. Some resources seem unlimited, while others, such as forests, are quickly disappearing. High-tech manufacturing occurs not far from where Mexican native peoples practice centuries-old traditions. The very rich live alongside people who live in extremely poor conditions. These situations create challenges that the Mexican people and government will need to address in the twenty-first century.

Too many people

People wonder how much longer Mexico can support its quickly growing population and the increasing number of people who live in poverty. Mexico is struggling to provide its citizens with services such as education, housing, health care, and unemployment benefits.

Rich and poor

More than half of Mexico's population lives in poverty. Many people cannot find steady work or work that pays a good wage. Rural areas are especially poor. Thousands of people have moved from the countryside to bigger cities in search of a better life. Unfortunately, Mexico's cities cannot provide for all the newcomers. Many of the immigrants end up living in shantytowns on the edge of the city. Other Mexicans migrate to the United States in search of work.

(opposite page, top) Factories are a major source of pollution in Mexico.

(below) Major Mexican cities are surrounded by poor areas called shantytowns.

Environmental concerns

Environmental problems are a growing cause for concern. Factory and automobile **emissions** pollute the air in the cities. Toxic waste from factories and raw sewage are dumped into rivers and lakes. Polluted air and water cause many Mexicans to become sick every year.

Air pollution

Millions of people in Mexico drive automobiles. Exhaust from all these vehicles, along with pollution from factories, has contributed to a thick layer of smog that hovers over each city. Laws limiting emissions from cars and factories and programs for public transportation have not been very effective in solving pollution concerns. Many citizens and organizations are working to fight pollution and raise awareness about Mexico's environmental problems.

Traditional ways

Mexico's native peoples have survived for thousands of years—through conquests, revolutions, and natural disasters. Some fear that their traditional ways will not survive in the face of today's rapidly changing world. Poverty, racism and discrimination, and lack of access to education are just some of the challenges faced by many Native Mexicans.

(below) Native people are trying to maintain their traditional way of life in modern Mexico.

Glossary

archaeologist A person who studies the past through buildings and artifacts

barren Unable to produce or support life

Bering Strait A channel of water that separates northeast Asia from northwest North America

bevy A large group of animals

biosphere An ecosystem; an area in which plant and animal life sustain each other

burro A small donkey

civilization A society with a well-established culture that has existed for a long period of time

coatamundi A raccoon-like animal found from the southern United States to South America

colonial Describing or relating to a land or people ruled by a distant country

constitution The set of laws that govern a country

deciduous Describing trees, such as the maple or oak, that lose their leaves in the winter

emigrate To leave one's home country and go to live in another country

emissions Substances, such as engine exhaust, that are sent out into the air

empire A group of countries under one ruler

fertile Able to grow many plants or crops

habitat The natural environment of a plant or animal

humid Moist; damp

hydroelectricity Electricity produced by waterpower

irrigate To water crops using artificial channels or streams that run through fields

Latin America The Spanish- or Portuguese-speaking countries of Central and South America

limestone Calcium-filled rock that is formed from decayed plants

margay A breed of small, spotted wildcat that lives in Mexico and Central and South America

metropolis A large city

migrate To move from one place to another

monument A structure dedicated to a person or event

natural resource Anything that exists in nature and is useful to human beings. Forests, mineral deposits, and water are all natural resources

New World The name given to North, South, and Central America by sixteenth-century explorers

oasis An area in a desert where plants are able to grow because there is a source of water

ocelot A breed of cat similar to the margay, but with a shorter tail and a narrower face

ore A naturally occurring mineral from which a metal is extracted

peninsula A point of land that juts into a body of water

plateau A flat, high-altitude landform

protein Chemicals that are necessary for growth and health, found in foods such as eggs, meat, and milk

refuge A place safe from danger

revolution A war in which the people of a country fight against the government

tapir A horselike tropical animal that sleeps during the day and is active at night

tarpon A large saltwater fish popular for eating

turbine An engine powered by a wheel that is turned by water, steam, or air

Index

1 2 3 4 5 6 7 8 9 0   Printed in the U.S.A.   9 8 7 6 5 4 3 2 1 0